THE MINDSET OF A GODLY WOMAN LIVING SINGLE IN A SECULAR WORLD!

THIS BOOK IS TO DELIVER, HEAL
AND RESTORE THOSE WHO ARE SEEKING GOD

GLORY

Order this book online at www.trafford.com
or email orders@trafford.com

Most Trafford titles are also available at major online book retailers.

Scripture quotations marked NIV are taken from the Holy Bible, New
International Version®. NIV®. Copyright © 1973, 1978, 1984 by International
Bible Society. Used by permission of Zondervan. All rights reserved.

Print information available on the last page.

ISBN: 978-1-4907-2846-9 (sc)
ISBN: 978-1-4907-2845-2 (e)

Trafford rev. 02/28/2015

Trafford PUBLISHING® www.trafford.com
North America & international
toll-free: 1 888 232 4444 (USA & Canada)
fax: 812 355 4082

This is a small but powerful book. In this book, there's healing for those who are broken, there's deliverance for those who need to be delivered, and there's restoration for those who need to be restored. You will read about some of my trials and tribulations that only God has taken me through. If you are in the need of God, come on a journey where you will have to face the reality of life, but note that God has his way of bringing you to the storm and delivering you through it. Now, it won't be easy, but God has used me to share my testimonies and help someone get their breakthrough through this page-turner! I also have a couple of my friends' testimonies in here to encourage you. By the time you finish reading this book, you will be uplifted, restored, inspired, and healed, all because of God's grace and mercy! I give God all the honor and glory because it was he who has been *Pulling Me Through*!

ACKNOWLEDGMENT

Special thanks to first and foremost God, He has been with me this whole journey. Next are my sisters Kesha you raised me to be a fighter and because of that I am a Survivor thank you for being there always and Chasity you are my cheerleader no matter how Big or Small my dream is you believe in it. I told you Tyler Perry was going to read this book and you just Cheered. Thank you for supporting me. And to my BFF Janaka M Barnes thank you for being there since day one there's so many pages you had to listen to and you did it with no problem, you encourage me and you helped me Spiritually along the way I am you and you are me , we are more than just friends it's a spiritual thing! To Felisha Thank you for being my Ride or Die many nights I had you up listening to my Dreams and Goals you took a chance and followed me to ATL not knowing what was going to happen you just believed in my dream and I love you so much for being there as I took that leap of Faith you are a major part of what God is doing in my life I Love you More!! I want to give a huge shout out to my brother Min Malcolm Barnes III, thank you for supporting the vision God has given me you have been there as a Role model and you have inspired me to keep Pushing no matter what I Love you Big Brother Soul Winner's For Life !!, I could say much more but time won't let. Special thanks to my Pastor Kevin Mitchell and First Lady Amanda F Mitchell for installing identity concepts in me, if it wasn't for you two and

God, I wouldn't know my worth or identity. I love you more than you can imagine. Thanks to my kingdom family CEWC for being a special part of my life, thank you Deacon Fred for reading and helping me get to this point in my book! And thank you to all who have made an impact in my life, I love you and there ain't nothing you can do about it and even if you try I'm still going to love you any way. Thanks to my adoptive parents Mrs. Toni K Jeanlouis and Mr. Eddie Sr Jeanlouis for taking me in and teaching me the value of having a relationship with God, Mrs . Toni it was you who told me to write this book you told me I had a testimony that some young lady needed to hear I Love You for seeing what I didn't see at the time. To Jaselyn, Jazzman ,Junior and Jarayha I love you all too the moon and back because ya'll allowed me to come in and be a part of ya'll family not to many kids would have done that. Last but not least to my kids Da'Laysha L Chassion and Shalil K Chassion you two are my motivators I Push so hard because of you two I Love You and we have so much to do in the Kingdom!!!

MESSAGE 1

You Leave a Man You Can See for a Man You Can't!

The best decision I ever made in my life was letting go of a man who I thought loved me. I was head over heels in love with him, and there wasn't anything I wouldn't do to keep him smiling. I thought he was the best thing God had created. I gave him all of me, and as a matter of fact, I lost myself in him! I couldn't see past him. No matter how many signs God showed me about him cheating me, I held on. No matter how many times he belittled me, I didn't leave him! I was caught up with this guy. I didn't want to accept the fact that he had changed. He wasn't the God-fearing man I had met, and somewhere along the way, he got lost in his situation and gave up on God and me. But I didn't want to believe that, so I kept on praying and hoping that he would come around and turn from his wicked ways. I kept on praying for my Prince Charming to return from his wicked ways, which never happened; he never came back but only got worse! One day, I woke up and asked myself, "What are you holding on to, Kendra? It is obvious that this man doesn't know your worth." Ladies, there's nothing worse than being in a relationship and feeling like you're not in one. I tried everything to make it work, but it wasn't for me to do. God had not planned for me and him to be together, and that was just that. I wasn't what he wanted. Sometimes, ladies, we have to realize that just because somebody walks out of our lives, it doesn't mean they deserted us. Some people are not meant to be together even though they have relations. I remember in one of Tyler Perry movies, Madea said, "When you have done all you could to make things work and the other person still doesn't meet you halfway, it's time to let them go!" Don't hold on to a pointless relationship. If you do, you're only wasting your time and energy. Move forward and learn from it. There's no reason to hold on to a man who doesn't want to hold on too. The worst feeling in a relationship is when you love and not being loved back! Horrible! Eventually, I made up my mind and walked away from this relationship. It was hurtful, and I cried many nights, but when I cried, I asked God to comfort me and make me whole again! I went back to my first love, and I let him mend the pieces of my broken heart. How much longer was I suppose to stay in a pointless relationship where I wasn't being treated like a queen. I would never forget the day when I asked my ex how much time he needed to realize that his life was not his own. You know, he looked at me in my eyes and said, "It's either God or me! You can't be with both of us." My heart dropped, but I looked at him in his eyes and told him, "*My Father will never leave me nor forsake like you!* But you, my love, the minute you feel like hopping to the next top model, you're going! So you say it's either you or God." Well, that day was the day I became single again! Ladies, never allow anyone to make you choose between your Father and them. That shouldn't even be an alternative anyway! I rather take my chances with the one I can't see. At least I know he loves me for me, and I don't have to lose out on anything for him to love me back. Ladies, one thing I have learned was *no man can replace god!* No man can love you like God, adore you, respect you, and encourage you. God is a friend to the friendless, a lover to the lonely, a healer to the sick, provider to all, and a mender to the brokenhearted! As I end this message, the song by Whitney Houston runs through my mind, "Where Do Broken Hearts Go!" Well, I have an answer to that question. We go to the one who first loved us, the one who pulled us out of the drug house, out of that abusive relationship, and out of that sinful life, and the one who never took his hands off you, even when you threw yours up at him. The Alpha and Omega, the one whose love is never ending, and the river of love just flow from him. His name is Jesus. The man I can't see but know he lives inside of me!

MESSAGE 2

Don't Confuse Your Path with Your Destination, Just Because It's Stormy!

I read the above-mentioned quote on You Tube one day, and it ministered to me, because the day I read it, my car had just run out of gas coming from work. It was approximately ninety-one degrees outside, and I was tired! The only money I had was my client's money and I knew I couldn't use that, so I began to get discouraged. I knew it was only a test, but I was tired and ready to go home and get ready for church. I sat in the car for a minute or so just thinking who I could get help from. I walked to the gas station and put gas in a gas can, and it wasn't enough, so I just said you know what, "Father, you handle this." I got out of the car and walked to my house. When I got home, I just fell on my couch and thanked God for giving me the strength to make it. I then called a friend of mine and asked her if she would take me to go put gas in my car. She said yes, so off we went, but before we got to my car, she pulled out five dollars and handed it to me and said, "Put this in your tank!" When I say "Favor," you can't tell me God isn't good. Back to the message, this incident inspired me to write this message, because some of us have gone through this or is going through this and you need to know that God is there. You have to trust him where you can't trace him! I didn't know this was going to happen to me, but it did teach me a valuable lesson: God will use anybody to help you. It doesn't matter if that person wants to do it or not, God said so, so shall it be! A lot of people are going through spiritual Welfare right now. Just because things are not the same anymore, we think our life is about to end, but it's not. This is just the beginning. God is shifting some things around to see how *faithful* you are, and I can tell you this because I'm going through this as I write. I had it all together once upon a time, and yes, God was my first priority, but like Job, I had to be tested. I had to endure some uncomfortable things and situations, where I never thought I would be. The fact is I was spiritually growing rapidly. He had to throw some obstacles in my path to test my faith! When I started, I confused my path with my destination because I thought I was stuck where I was. I didn't think I was going to get out or be moved higher. The places where my car ran out of gas and the times my lights got turned off because I didn't have the money to pay, it was just the things I had to go through for God to show me that he is *able*. I couldn't run to any of my friends or family, so what was the next option? Christ! I messed up by making Christ my last option when he should have been my first. I wouldn't have gone through so much, but it was for God's use! When I began to grow with God, I realized that as I was going through, God had been holding my hand every step of the way and that my finances may not be growing now, but my spiritual walk was. I am getting closer to my Father and learning to trust him in all I go through, no matter how big or small it is. You see, my destination is me coming out of my storm wherever God has me. Once I'm out, that's where I stand, and it doesn't have to be a place; it could be your relationship with him. Kingdom, you may be going through a storm right now, but that doesn't mean your sunshine is not near. First Lady Amanda Mitchell always quotes: "Just because you're delayed doesn't mean you're denied!" And another quote she likes to say, "It may not be God-sent, but it will be God-used." Trust God, stand on his word, keep on praising him, and keep on pressing toward him. The rain is not going to last for long! Have faith, for we know that faith moves the hands of God! And remember, don't confuse your path for your destination, because where God is taking you is totally different from where he's leaving you! Praise him!

MESSAGE 3

I Don't Want a Relationship with Man When I Can Have an Encounter with Christ!

When I wrote this message, I decided to make my point very direct. The title simply states, "I don't want a relationship with man when I can have an encounter with Christ!" Some people might be saying, "Oh, she's saying that because she's single. Now, let some fine, sexy, dark man approach her, she'll think twice!" (Worldly thinkers!) I'm not saying that I don't ever want a relationship with a man. I'm simply pointing out that as women, we tend to make it our business to have a relationship with any man. I was once that woman! I left God for a man who I thought was my happily ever-after and found he was my Jason/Freddie! If you get what I'm saying, a relationship with a man can go two ways: good or bad. And if you're thinking with your mind and not following the Spirit, you will end up with a bad man, someone who has no interest in you at all. He would not even see you in his future and you might be the best thing that ever happened to him. But he's a double-minded man. He is unstable in all his ways, so he doesn't know how to treat you because he doesn't know your value. Ladies, you want a man who's chasing after God's own heart, a man who's not afraid to worship God, and the one who will pull you toward God, not from him. You don't want to be with a man or woman who has no morals, faith, values, or respect! You better do like Madea says, "Runnn!" Because a man or woman like that is about to drag you into all kinds of confusion, and where there is confusion, there's no God. My pastor often says, *The devil can't stay where he's not welcome.* So, if you're dating someone who is inviting the devil into your life, you need to let them go! Never give the devil easy access to take your peace. Give him a challenge. The devil can't just steal from me anymore. He has a fight on his hands. I have been through too much to allow him to just take from me easily. Like the title says, I rather have an encounter with Christ than a pointless relationship with man, especially with one who can't even pray with me or tell me what I mean to him, excuse me for saying this, but *no invaders*! I speak strongly on this because there're some women out there who think having a piece of man is better than having no man at all. Betty Wright didn't know her identity at the time she sung that song. She didn't realize the poison she was putting into people's ear! Having an encounter with Christ is an awesome feeling. It's like you start thinking what was I thinking settling for 80 percent when God is 100 plus! When you encounter with Christ, that wisdom and knowledge you were looking for will appear and that joy and peace you couldn't find will be there suddenly! First Lady Amanda likes to say, *I rather be in God's will than in his way*! If God is doing something in your life, let him and don't care how slow the process looks, keep it moving! I know you're lonely, but I think you're only as lonely as you think you are. Spirit over Mind—God is always there. I tell you this, if you want a relationship, have one with Jesus, and I promise you'll never have another lonely night!

MESSAGE 4

When Will You Let God In

The steps of a good man are ordered by the Lord and he delighted in his way. Though he fall, he shall not utterly cast down, for the Lord upholdeth him with his hand. (Ps. 37:23–24).

"When will you let God in?" I asked a friend of mine this question a thousand times. He kept on going in circles, without knowing which way to go or who to turn to. He was very scared of change but wanted to live a life of luxury. He would rather go through the motions of chasing after different girls trying to find the next top model and lose himself. He said he wanted to find a woman who loved him for what he was. My question to him was "Who are you? How can a woman love you for you when you don't even know who you are?" That just didn't make any sense. I could remember when he was in a situation where he was with a female who said she loved him and he gave her his all. Well, he happened to go to jail, and she packed her and her kids' belongings and forgot all about him. Before the judge could have sentenced him, she had skipped town with her children's father! Wow, now where's the loyalty! He got mad with God. When that happened, he couldn't understand why all that was happening to him. I told him, "We served a jealous God. No man can come before him. He shares his glory with no one, and you were giving all of you to the wrong person." We as people, put too much into others instead of God. I realized that man will always let you down. No matter how much you put into that person, if they're not for you, they're not going to be there when times get hard. Romans 8:28 states, "And we know that god causes everything to work together for the good of those who love god and are called according to his purpose for them." So if that woman was meant to be in his life, she wouldn't have left his side so fast and easily. T. D. Jakes once said, "If it's easy for a person to walk out of your life, then they weren't destined to be in your future." We as people try to make people fit into our lives when there's really no room for them. God has a way of stopping us from destroying our own lives. He will put things in our way to keep us from making bad decisions that we will regret later. If my friend would have looked at his situation spiritually, he would have seen that God was only keeping him from getting into more trouble than he was and that he didn't lose on anything, not even the years of not seeing his daughter because God has the power to restore things. For all that time he spent away from his daughter, God could put them in each other's lives and he won't even notice what he had missed because God likes to restore the years and make things better than before! I learned that people will leave you. You should never put your all in someone who is not promised to you. Take your all and invest it into God. He is the one whom you can trust your all with!

MESSAGE 5

Never Mistake Your Assignment for Your Boaz

One who is gracious to a poor man lends to the Lord,
and he will repay him for his good deed.(Prov. 19:17)

Some people of the opposite sex are placed in our lives only for a season. God has a purpose for all of us to fulfill, and if you're walking in his will, he will put some folks in your life for you to be what I like to call "Their Open Bible." This means some people are scared to go to church, because they feel that they have to live in a certain way to be a part of the congregation if they only knew if they all do it all together they wouldn't need God then God wouldn't get his Glory and we all know that's not about to happen. God will use you and me as his disciples in training to speak the word to his lost sheep, and you living in a secular world and still fighting your flesh have to recognize your purpose in this person's life. For example, say you meet a guy who had been broken in every area of his life. What all he once had which is all he has nothing now. So you come across him and the two of you connect. You both will begin talking over the phone, and next you know you both are the perfect couple, so you'll say! What happened to introducing him to God's Disciple? How you went from being on an *assignment* to becoming involved with a man? That's what many of us single Godly woman do. We forget that just because he is a good man and single doesn't mean he's our man. Your job was to get him to the church and not in your heart. Your job is done on to your next assignment. Don't make something that is intended to be seasonal *permanent*. You are getting into God's way, and you don't want to be in God's way when he has a purpose for that person. Remember, be lead by the Spirit and not your feelings. We as people often feel that we can take things into our own matters. That person doesn't need us; They need God. They are not seeking to be put together. What they really need is time with God. They are broken and hurt and need guidance, so never take it into your own hands. God uses us to do his works. He needs us to perform the duty because he's working beside the scene. Ladies, please don't mistake your assignment for your Boaz because you might just be getting in God's way. If he or she is meant for you, then trust me, God will let you know. Keep your eyes on God and your mind focus on his will. Remember, if you're seeking him and only him, you won't be easily distracted because God will help you along the way.

MESSAGE 6

Worldly Love Loves nobody
but Godly Love Does!

But, God commendeth his love toward us in that
while we were yet, sinners Christ died for us.
(Rom. 5:8)

Have you ever heard the song "Nobody Greater" by Vashawn Mitchell? Well, I would listen to it often and would sing it because I liked it, but I actually sat down in my home and listened to the lyrics of that song. When I became true to myself and allowed God to have complete control over my life, things just didn't make sense. "I searched all over, couldn't find nobody," the song says. I was giving a man all of me and getting none of him. I was taking care of a man trying to show him I was the one, when I wasn't his one! I looked high and low but still couldn't find anybody on the Internet, blind dates, etc . . . still no man there to love me. Yeah they loved the heck out of me in the bed. All he would hear is I love you, I would never hurt you, but what happened to my Spirit? The body/flesh was pleased, but my spirit was missing so much I thought a man would complete me, but how when they were never whole? Let's keep real. I know I was not by myself when I spent countless nights crying myself to sleep just because he didn't call or text me. Finally, when he did, it would not be more than two words. To whom was he speaking to? If you are a Spiritual person, please don't yoke yourself up with a person who doesn't have respect for the Christ in you. You have to think that how a person who is rejecting the Christ who lives in you will accept you. A person who doesn't have a personal relationship with Christ will never understand you because you're talking about Kingdom and he is talking about the trash; these two will never mix. Worldly people don't know what genuine love is. Their love is based on what they see and that's not very much. There's a love I can tell you about, although that's indescribable and incomparable. That love cannot be defined! And that's the *love of God*! Only God can love you through your mess and not judge you. He loves you no matter how many times you reject him. You can't find that type of love in the people. No Way! Be wise! Kingdom people know the difference between the two. Nobody is greater, nobody is greater, nobody is greater than you! No other *love I know*!

MESSAGE 7

Don't Miss the Kingdom Bus Carrying All That Baggage!

Be kind and compassionate to one another, forgiving
each other, just as in Christ God forgave you.
(Eph. 4:32)

I chose the heading of this chapter from a message I received on New Year's Day, and it really touched me. At that time, I was in church only physically, but my mind was on how I was starting the New Year in a relationship but in it by myself. I kept on telling myself, "Kendra, you're not going to take any shortcuts this year. It's either he get it together or you leave him." Was I fooling myself? As a matter of fact, even if I left him, I knew deep down in my heart that he would just move on to the next woman, and I believe that was why I settled for so less because I knew deep down in my heart that it wouldn't mattered if I was in his life or not. I know right what was I thinking hooking up with a person who care less of how they made me feel, but to get back. We as ladies carry a lot of hurt, pain, disappointments, brokenness, and our list goes on and on. It's always through someone who we love dearly, someone who we trust, and someone who we told all our secrets to. And what we do is we hold on to all that bitterness, and it piles up, not going anywhere but changing everything about ourselves, and then we're at a standstill in our life, not moving forward at all. You gave that person power to hold you down, and they don't even know it and probably wouldn't care if they did. You were once a joy to be around; now, you're always sad, upset, and ready to jump on somebody's case. How did you get there? I can tell you because I had been there. You're so busy hurting and you don't even realize you're hurting yourself. Kingdom, if you're going to hurt, hurt, but don't let it go as far as you're hurting yourself. You can ask, "How can you do that?" Well, I am happy you asked. It is by thinking about those nights he left you home to be with another woman, or the night when you tried to make him stay and he still walked out the door. Maybe you're thinking about the times you cried yourself to sleep because it was two in the morning and he was not home and did not answering any of your phone calls. Ladies, don't do that to yourself if you want to move forward and be joyful. You have to know when to stop mourning. T. D. Jakes in one of his books had said that heartache is like a funeral. You cry at the service, but when you get to the burial, it's time to realize that person is gone and you have to leave them there, which means you have to let them go. It doesn't mean you have to forget them. It just means you have to let go and allow God to fill in. He also had said not to stay at the burial for too long. Don't hinder yourself. Allow God to touch what has been broken; instead of holding on to that baggage, let it go. It doesn't serve any purpose in your life. Take this time and enjoy being single. Get closer to God, and if you don't have one with him, by all means get one and let him show you the true meaning of *I will never leave you nor forsake you*. Let God show you the way you're supposed to be loved, and don't get into another relationship carrying all that baggage because all you're going to do is hurt the next person. 1 John 2:15 states, "Do not love the world or the things in the world. If anyone loves the world, the love of the Father is not in them." This means you have to love God first before loving a man or woman. How can you love a man or a woman first anyway when you don't love the Creator who created the man, that same person you love? Moreover, you're not healed. A broken heart is like a sore; it needs time to heal. When you cut yourself, won't you apply some medicine on it? In this case, God is your medicine; instead of healing only on the outside, he's going to start from the inside first and then would heal the outside wound. There are certain wounds which you can't cover and hence, it won't heal completely. A bad breakup is similar to these wounds. You can't just cover this wound by jumping into another relationship. It's not going to change how your heart feels. You have to let God work on the inside of you, let him clean your heart and treat it, and let him heal you from the pain so that it can become a scar. You don't want to miss the Kingdom Bus carrying all that baggage. Ladies and gentlemen, don't become a victim. "Let Go and Let God"! If someone has hurt you or are hurting you, remove them out of your life because they don't belong to the place where God is taking you. My pastor always tells us in our Single's Meetings, "If he or she is your past, they were there for a reason. Stop looking backwards and look what's ahead of you." You're trying to change someone who you can't change and who doesn't want to change. Then he says, "Who are you to try to change a man when God can only do that!" Daughter, Son, don't allow breakups to be the reason you miss the Kingdom Bus. Don't get stuck living in your past with all that baggage! Get on the bus and make it to Kingdom Land!

MESSAGE 8

The Devil Sets Traps but God Sets Blessings

I once met one of my cousins, and we were just talking about all the things she had gone through as a child, a teenager, and an adult. Now, did you catch I said *gone through*? This means she had come out of it! Anyways she was telling how as a child she got molested and turned to drugs to numb her pain. She lost sight of herself, and she turned to the streets. Her mother looked after her kids. She began to be in and out of jail as a matter of routine! She felt the only way to be loved was to be with a man, so she dedicated herself to men, which made her situation more worse. Then what? She was empty inside not realizing all she had to do was turn to Christ. I think we all have been through something dramatic where it's either we deal with it head on or run and hide from it. Well, at least we think we're hiding, but our actions tell a different story. As she was telling me her testimonies, all I could relate to was a scripture from Ezekiel 3:19. It states, "Yet if thou warn the wicked, and he turn not from his wickedness, nor from his wicked way, he shall die in his iniquity, but thou hast delivered thy soul." You see, she was living an unstable and double-minded life, with no cares in the world. Even in her sin, God's mercy fell upon her, and he saved her from her own sin that could have killed her! The devil wanted to keep her empty. He didn't want anything positive to nurture that hurt and disappointment she carried. You see, the devil plays games and one of them is "Ring Around Your Life." He will have you go through the same circle with no change in your life. He can have you running back to the same man who just put his hands on you and tell you he loves you, but he will do only that. The enemy likes to be unstable. He hates correction and order. He's misery, and he wants company. Don't allow yourself to be a part of his company. You have to be strong and realize Kingdom. We don't do circles; we do triangles! Ladies, I repeat, don't allow your circumstances keep you in bondage. Your life will pass by. Time waits for no one. Don't let anybody take your years away from you, and when you're old, you want them back. My cousin was in bondage, and it was when she went to prison that she almost lost her mind and changed her mind. She decided not to go to man but to The Man! She got her life together, and when she came home, God gave her a chance to be a mother to her two children. He gave her, her womanhood back. She found her worth. You see, the devil set her *trap*, but God set her *blessing*. God gave her everything that the devil stole from her. He restored the years and gave her another chance to live right. *What a mighty God we serve. He's so merciful and loving, no wonder his love is called Agape!* There's nothing too hard for him!

MESSAGE 9

Sweet Talker, Pipe Dream Maker!

Ladies, yes, I went there! Did I catch your attention? Yep, I knew I had.

I knew I wouldn't be the only one who could relate to this message. We all have been through our share of sweet talkers and pipe dream makers! Tell me this, ladies, did you learn from them, or did you fall from them? You see you can meet someone, and everything outward about him is wonderful but everything inside is dead: no life, no spirit, no love, and just darkness. This makes me think about the saying, "Everything that glitters ain't gold." You really have to know who you're dealing with. You have to know what that person's motives are in your life. There's no use in just allowing someone to take up space in your life for nothing. A lot of us who are single fall victim to this, because we never got love at home as a child, so when we get older, we look for it in a man, which's not the case. It's not love, and it's really lust! God is *love*. Know that. Listen, young ladies, I've been there, so I know what I'm talking about. I'm not just speaking about this without any experience. Now, let me introduce the sweet talker. He is the one who's going to tell you everything you want to hear and not what you need to hear only because his motives are not for you. He's going to send you flowers unannounced and surprise you with candy and material things because he figures that that's what you want. Then within four months, he will change. He will start showing his real self. Be careful, ladies, he's going to use your likes against you. Yes, I know it sounds crazy, but he will use everything that you had told him you like to lure you to make sure he's for you and not against you. Allow God to place your Boaz in your life. That way, you will know if he's God-sent and hence there won't be any drama. A sweet talker will talk you right out of your identity. Be very careful, Kingdom! Watch who you let in your heart! Ladies and gentlemen, listen to me when I say, *Never let someone make you their option.* You should be their choice and not the second either. The devil is a skimmer. Remember he didn't go to Eve as a snake. He went to her in a way she would be comfortable listening to him. Read Genesis 3 1–5! A pipe dreamer will tell you this and that and will never live up to his promise. He will tag you along for years and mess up your credit. He will take your money so you'll be working to take care of him and his needs and treat you like second best. And that's his dream for a woman to take care of him and treat him like a king, something he's far from. Ladies, there are men out there who claim to be something or someone they are not. Don't be surprised they are out there! Keep your eyes on God. You won't need the worldly man's dream, because God gave you a vision of your own. Just stand firm and in the will of God.

MESSAGE 10

Loyalty Is Earned. Stop Giving It Away So Easily!

I decided to talk about loyalty because a lot of men and women are being loyal to the wrong people. Being loyal to someone is not easy. You have to really love that person, and they must really have proven their self to you. Before, a person doesn't need to do much to prove himself to me so that I will be loyal to him. What I didn't realize was that I was being loyal to people who didn't deserve it. Their motives in my life were pointless. They had no intentions in helping to lead a better life. Even they had no intentions of staying with me. The first person I should have been loyal to was God; instead, I was loyal to man. I once was watching a reality show. A female and male in that show was on and off in a relationship, but for the most part, they were out. Well, in this one episode that I watched, the man went to jail and the female thought the judge was giving him some time so she went adjusted the engagement ring that he gave to her not knowing that he was getting out soon, and when he did, she went and told him what she had done before his mother would go and tell him. Well, when she pulled him to the side and told him she blew his mind, he got upset and told her she wasn't loyal to him. How can you be loyal to someone who is cheating on you? Okay, you proposed to her, but you were still messing with your ex. How can you expect someone to be loyal to a disloyal person? Listen, fellas, it's only so much a woman will take. Sooner or later, your games would be boring and we will move on. There's no way you can do whatever you want to do and leave the woman just sitting and waiting until you're ready to be faithful. He was hurt about it. I could see it in his face, but the more I watched this show, I thought to myself how loyal he was to her. You know, me being the woman that I am now, I would have been upfront with him and would have given his ring back to him instead of adjusting it. I would have waited until it was me and him. They were at a party when she told him about that which messed up his whole night. God should have been a factor in both of their lives and the drama that they were going through. They should have settled it together. I actually wish I could encourage them both to allow God in their lives, but one thing I noticed was that the male's mother was supposed to be his anchor and she gave him a lot of advice that caused him a lot of drama. My advice to him is, "Go to God with your problems because your momma is giving you the wrong advice. She is pulling you from God and not toward him." Loyalty is earned and not just given away!

MESSAGE 11

When You Let Go of What No Longer Fits in Your Life, You Will Have Room for What God Wants There!

Hey, ladies, this chapter comes from Romans 8:28. It states, "And we know that all things work together for the good to them that love God, to them who are called according to his purpose." Sometimes we as women hold on ask him Father what I am doing so wrong. Well, let me tell you I'm glad you asked. First, you went looking for him, and he was supposed to find you. When he did find you, it was supposed to be in your worship. We as women tend to think God is taking too long to send our Boaz, and we try to move ahead of him not realizing that God knows what is best for us. We make a lot of decisions based on our flesh; hence, really, there's no way of seeing the mistake we make. Your flesh is battling with your Spirit because you say yes and God says no! You don't know if it's right or wrong. Now, think about the last time you went to God regarding a problem. Didn't he give you an answer, and wasn't it the right answer? Well, why the answer is wrong when you answer it yourself? It's like when God blesses you with a raise in your job, you take it upon yourself to go and buy you a brand-new car with a high note. Now, you know you have other bills to be paid, but because you want something new and you got a raise, you feel it's only the right thing to do. Like, really, did you pray before making that decision? You didn't need God's input at that time, did you? We as people have to be careful not to get ahead of ourselves. *Too much is given much is required* are mindful of your lifestyle. Well, holding on to a guy who is pointless in your life is just like buying a car you didn't need to. Stop adding people who do not belong to you into your life. If you keep doing that, then you won't have time for the people who belong to you because you will be too busy trying to figure out why this one and that one are there in your life. Save yourself the headache! Some of us keep people in our lives so that we are not alone. That's the wrong reason to hold on to somebody when all they do is get whatever they want from you and never there to help you in the time of need. Just think how can God bless you when you have this person right there ready to suck up all your blessings? You need to be connected to people who mean something and who actually wants to see you elevate and not stay at bottom! T. D. Jakes said one day, "If it's easy for a person to wall out of your life, then it means they weren't destined to be in your destiny." Stop trying to keep people in your life who don't fit and make room for those who do!

MESSAGE 12

They Didn't Walk Away From You

I decided to write about this because a lot of people actually become bitter when someone walks away from them, thinking that it was a problem with them. You see, I was in a relationship where this happened to me. I thought my ex had walked away from me, but actually, he walked away from God. You see, even though he had hurt me, I still wanted him to be a part of my life. I couldn't understand why would I still want him, and he had brought heartache to me. Well, it occurred to me that once he texted me and started apologizing for how things ended, he had realized that I was very Spiritual and he wasn't. At first, I wasn't hearing that, I mean seriously was that all you could come up with? Those were the thoughts that ran through my mind, how do you hurt someone Spiritual like me. We were together for nine months no matter what I did with you, God was still in me. As a matter of fact, he told me I was the first Spiritual woman he had been with, but God is all I can say. I felt like he had walked away from us. To me, he didn't fight and he didn't try to change for the sake of the love I thought we had for each other. I couldn't understand why someone I loved so much would just leave me. Then I began to move on and got me together. Holy Spirit revealed to me that it wasn't he who walked away and it wasn't he who gave up on us, but God had removed him! Why? Let me tell you. I was chasing after a man's heart when I should have been chasing after God. I spent hours and days planning out our day to him not even caring about how my hair looked or the clothes I had on. I was chasing after a man who had no clue about the worth of God, so surely, he didn't know the worth of our love. That was why it was easy for him to find someone else because there was no feelings. And waited for nine months before he left. The signs were always there. I just didn't want to see them. God always gives us cautious signs. Holy Spirit had showed me that he was unfaithful because I caught him cheating. So God had to let me go through the pain because I didn't want to take heed. There are so many like this and I know I'm not by myself on this! You see, sometimes we as people, we take God's purpose and we make it our purpose. God started showing me that the purpose in my ex life wasn't for him to be my boyfriend, but for him to see the God in me. I took my assignment for my Boaz. Big Mistake, and that's another message for you to read. The whole time I was in my relationship, I was moving away from God. I started having sex, and I got out of God's will. What I learned is you don't want to do that. It's easy for the devil to attack you. I couldn't see the hindrance, the misguided love; as a matter of fact, the love became a road block because my walk very strong that the devil used my relationship to distract me. I was busy trying to make it work with a man who didn't want to put in work. We as single people get lonely and are ready to enter into a relationship as soon as the opposite sex presents them. I failed to see that my relationship that I wanted so badly was blocking my walk with God. God couldn't take me to the next level because my mind wasn't right and wasn't mature enough. For sure, my ex wasn't ready for where God was taking me, and it would have never worked. Holy Spirit said, "Be of good cheer. He has a new thing awaiting me at the next level, so keep moving." God kept me from missing out on the next level of my walk! Thank you, Lord for being my strength when I was weak! People don't walk away from you for just no reason. God removes them so he can do what he has to do in your life. Count it all joy!

Poem 1

I'm Still Here!

I've been lied on, but I'm still here

I've been talked about, but I'm still here

I've been counted out, but I'm still here

I've been told that I would never amount to anything, but I'm still here

I've been mistreated, but I'm still here

Through it all the devil tried to make me give up!

I've been abused, but I'm still here

I've been cursed, but I'm still here

I've been cheated on, but I'm still here

I've been used, misused, and reused, but I'm still here

I didn't allow what I went through bring me down!

I've been down, but I'm still here.

God didn't let me go! No matter what others may have said or did, I made it! And I'm Still Here!

MESSAGE 13

Where Do Our Kids Go When We As Parents Don't Validate Them!

Train up a child in the way he should go and when
he is old he will not depart from it. (Prov. 22:6)

The scripture says train up a child and not train down a child in the way he should go. The title of this message is the reason why I picked this scripture.

I can relate to the message because I grew up without having a mother or father. My mom died when I was thirteen years old, and my dad was never around. My oldest sister raised me until I moved out of her house when I was sixteen years old. I then went and stayed with some friends. From the eyes of everybody, my life as a teenager became invisible, and I started living as a young adult. The reason why I say this is because even though I stayed with friends, I had to fend for myself. My best friend's mother tried to help as much as she could, but eventually, things didn't work out there. It wasn't until my family counselor took me in with her family. I was the oldest there, and we actually would fuss as if we were all actually sisters. Lol! I could remember the time the youngest and I was going at it, and I was so mad at her, but the love was a sisterly love because we shared the same room so I couldn't be mad at her for long. And the oldest and I were tight. We shared a lot together, and we pretty much got along too. My adoptive mother raised me to have respect for myself, and she taught me how to take care of myself. She showed me the values of life and kept me in church and for the most part in the Bible. I thank *God* for her because she took me in not knowing how things would go and not too many people would do that. Now to get back to the message, I want to make this clear that all adults take this information in love. I'm not trying to tell you how to raise your child or kids or am I trying to take sides because just like you, I have been on both sides. I am daughter of a woman and I am a mother of a daughter, so I know what we as parents go through on a daily basis. I just wanted to allow us as parents to see our kid's point of view without fussing, cursing, and yelling, just simply taking it in and putting ourselves in their shoes. Okay, I did some talking with several teens at my job at the juvenile detention home, and I found some awesome but disturbed kids. I talked to one of them and asked her several questions about why do they do what they do. One question I asked her was, "Why would a young girl like herself walk the streets late at night instead of being in her warm home?" The second question was why she felt that her mother/father didn't love her. Her answer to the first question was that when she's walking the streets at night, she's with her boyfriend and that the reason she sneaks out is because her mother doesn't accept him. I asked her, "Well, why don't she accept him? Is he disrespectful or too old for you? Does he have his pants hanging to the ground looking like a fool, or what?" She replied yes to all. Then as I was about to comment, she said, "At least he loves me!"

I thought to myself, "Wow!" I told her, "You're telling me, because this young man is telling you he loves you, you're being rebellious to your mom." She said, "Yes, and I don't care how you look at me, because you're not walking in my shoes!" So I looked at her and said, "Well, take me on your journey and explain to me how are you walking." She turned to me and said, "How can you learn to do right when your mother is calling you names like 'you're a woman in the streets,' and your daddy is telling you, 'you're just like your mother, a fool!'" Tears begin to fall from her eyes, and I looked at her and said, "Baby, it's not what they call you, it's what you answer to. Just because people go around calling you things doesn't mean you have to accept it. You have a choice and that is to prove them wrong. You know, earlier you told me I'm not walking in your shoes. Well, you were wrong. I have walked in your shoes before. Guess what? I didn't let what people thought or say about me become me, because I knew I was somebody! And the way you're going about your hurt and pain is going to lead you to where they are saying you will be." She started telling me about her life. She was a loving child who had been through some things and didn't know how to deal with it. The words that ran through my head as I listened to her was from the Bible which says, "Train up a child." Today some of us parents are not training up our kids. The minute they do something that's not right, we're tiring them down, instead of encouraging them and helping them get back on the right path. You see, as parents, we have to let our children know when the world rejects them that we have already accepted them. That's what God has done for us. God always let us know that even though we fall short of his glory, he loves us in the midst of our mess! That's how we have to love our kids. They don't just wake up one morning and say, "I want to be a prostitute," or "I want to be a drug dealer." It's something that has caused them to turn to the wrong way. It's our duty to pick them up and lead them to Christ and back on the right path. We can't just sit back and lose them to the streets to the enemy because we're going through our own mess. No! We have to fight to get them back. Some parents don't realize that the words that come out of our mouths is either *life* or *death*, so as a parent, we have to be careful what we speak into our kid's lives. Telling them that they are going to be B's and H's is not going to build them up; however, telling them that they can be anything they want as long as they have Christ will not only build them up but also they will have a relationship with Christ! No child, no matter how bad they are, are deserved to be put down. I used to fuss and curse and yell until I realized that was not going to make them do right. You have to kneel down and pray. In today's society, in this new generation, we have to pray without ceasing because they are not scared anymore. They are bold, and you would think they have been here before. We as parents, we get caught up being a grown up that we forget to nurture and love our kids. We can't just provide food, shelter, and water; we have to provide love, attention, and affection too. Mothers and fathers, you don't want the streets to show your child or children what love is. Catch them now and validate them. Pray for our kids and don't stop no matter how much trouble they are getting into. Remember, *Much prayer much power! No prayer no Power!* And to end this message, I would advice all mothers and fathers to take the first step to bettering their relationship with their kids by sitting them down and finding out what is going through their minds. Be a friend and love them. Let them know that you're there for them not just as a parent but as a friend too. The young girl took my advice and went to her mother with her problems, and as she opened up to her mother, she opened her mother's eyes too, and they are now working on their mother and daughter relationship. Her father fell right in line once he saw the difference in her. You see, prayer really works. We have to start praying, parents! God bless!

MESSAGE 14

To Get Over Old Love, Get New Love!

Ladies and gentlemen, I don't know if any of you had heard the cliché "To get over old love, get new love." I had heard, and listen to me when I say it's dead wrong! One thing I have learned in many relationships is that you must allow yourself time to heal. There's no sense in getting into another relationship and still going through the hurt and disappointment from the last one. I have seen many women including myself jump from relationship to relationship just to ease the pain, but in fact, all you're doing is getting into more pain because this guy might hurt you more worse than the previous one. Ladies, all you're doing is covering up that pain that you don't want o deal with. And I must tell you this, the only person that can heal you from a heartache is God because we as women, we give so much to a man when we are in a relationship that when it doesn't work out, we need to be replenished. We gave up so much like our heart, time, morals, respect, dignity, and independence, and God has to give that back to us. Some of us give up our walk and our calling to please our mate. So you see, finding new love is not going to make you better. It's only going to cover up the pain."To get over old love is to get new love" is a lie, a set up from the devil to get more distracted than you were before because you go through more hurt and in circles. There are no scars but only open wounds that are covered, and it shouldn't be because it needs to be treated! So you're thinking how it can be treated. It is by allowing yourself time to go through the process of finding yourself and learning to enjoy you all by yourself. Give yourself time with God. Let God's love on you nurture you and show you how you're supposed to be treated. Love doesn't hurt. It wasn't meant to hurt. God didn't create love for it to be a painful experience. He is love, so why would it hurt? Allow God to usher into your life and turn that bitterness into joy. You see, God is a mender of all broken hearts. Psalms 34:18 states that the Lord is near the broken-hearted, which means you're not alone because he's with you. At night, when you start feeling lonely, open your Bible and read the word or put on some worship music until you're ready to go to sleep. Then pray and ask God to comfort you, and trust me, he will. Psalms 25:16 states, "Turn to me and be gracious to me, for I am lonely and afflicted." You see, it tells us that he is there to comfort us. God has never asked us to do anything by ourselves, so why would he let us go through the hurt and pain by ourselves? Our Father is a loving Father. He keeps all his promises. The scriptures says, "The Lord is near the brokenhearted and saves those who are crushed in Spirit." Now that's a loving Father! Ladies, you don't need a man or men. You don't need a woman to complete you to make you whole. That's what God is for. Let him restore the pieces of your broken heart. He's there just waiting for you to come to him with it!

MESSAGE 15

He Wants His Glory

As I sat in church one Wednesday, pastor was preaching out of 2 Corinthians chapter 6, and as he began to teach, the Holy Spirit started leading him into a whole new direction. He went to say that, "They can touch you, but they can't touch you!" We at my church like to say, "Now, that was a Kingdom Shift!" Now let me explain to you just what he meant when he said that. When people try to bring up your past because they see you're changing and that nothing is getting to you, they begin to throw things in your direction to distract you to make you feel like you can't move from your past, but you have to stay strong. Kingdom, don't allow folks that are intimidated by the new you to throw your past in your face. They are just trying to distract you from where God is taking you. Psalms 51:10 says, "Create in me a clean heart O God and renew in me a right Spirit within me." Now, one thing I know is that when you use the word "right," there is *power!* Let me explain, anytime there's *Praise and Worship,* the devil is scared because he knows in Praise and Worship, God himself is in the midst. Whatever you maybe going through and whatever that has been holding you and keeping you in bondage has *got to be destroyed*! The devil knows that in Praise and Worship, chains are broken, lives are set Free, and people receive deliverance. He doesn't like that. Pastor taught us that "Praise" is in your right hand and "Worship" is in your left hand. You see, the two of them together will drive the devil away! Praise and Worship is what we call it, we use the weapon of righteousness in the right hand for the attack and the left hand to defeat! Which is when Praise and Worship has no point of return, it's just you and God and that is an awesome feeling people could be in and out of church you won't even hear or notice because you're in a place where you're hearing a Sound not the Noise that is surrounding you. God is so loving. His heart is so pure. It makes me wonder if I would ever meet someone like him. Umm . . . No! If you want to get out of some stuff, start to Praise and Worship God. That's your weapons to defeat whatever obstacles the devil throws at you! Have faith in all things James 2:14 states that faith without work is dead, which means if there's no Praise and Worship, you're not working and you're not believing; if you don't believe, then you don't trust God. To trust God is to go through things without knowing how you're going to come out of it, but you know, God is with you. My Pastor likes to say, "Trust God where you can't trace him!" Mary has a song that says, "Why should I think small when my God is big." He's bigger than just music. He controls the sound as a matter of fact and he lives inside of the person ministering the music, so why limit yourself? That's like winning a million dollars and living in a shack. Kingdom, you have someone Greater living inside of you, and you have to trust him at his word. God wants his glory, and he won't share it with anyone. It is he who pulled you out of that crack house. It is he who saved you from that abusive relationship. It is he who gave you that voice to sing and that dance that touch lives! None of that is you. It's all him. He created dance. He created your voice. Give him his glory. He deserves it! Praise him for what he has done and for what he is going to do. Praise him in Spirit and in truth. Let your worship be for real. You see in the word "Praise," there's the word "raise," so your hands should be raised at all time. This means "you're coming out!" Kingdom, be encouraged, stay focused, and know who lives inside of you. It's funny how people say, "Watch what spirit jump on you," but not in you, because darkness and light can't dwell in the same place. He wants his glory, and all you can do is allow him to use you, so he can get it!

Poem 2
Lord Please Restore the Pieces of My Broken Heart!

Lord, please restore the pieces of my broken heart. Take what man broke and thought didn't matter and make it brand new.

So I could stop crying. So I could stop hurting. Lord, please take me from this misery and place it with joy and laughter. In the places where there's a void, fulfill it with your love. For I know that you would never hurt me, never leave me, and would carry me through the waves of my life. Lord, please restore the broken pieces of my heart. I know I made mistakes including placing man before you, but if you could just take this pain away! I promise I'll never do it again, Lord, please restore the pieces of my broken heart. Every time I do it, I get the same results holding on to a pointless relationship hoping that my love would see us through. The lies cut like a knife and the thought of him not loving me is driving me. Lord, please take this unstable feeling and throw it back into the pits of hell. Lord, please restore the pieces of my broken heart, then I can let go. Set me free from the dreams, phone calls, and text messages. Set me free from the pictures that I carry in my heart. Lord, please restore the pieces of my heart, so I can experience your true love. Lord, please restore the pieces of my broken heart so these tears that fall from my eyes can fade away. Lord, please restore the pieces of my broken heart so I can Love once again!

MESSAGE 16

Position versus Purpose

Do you have a position in someone's life or a purpose? That's the question I'm asking both men and women. You never want to have a position but no purpose in someone's life, especially if you have strong feelings for them. If all they want is a friendship, then leave it at that. Know your boundaries and keep it that way. And a lot of men like to say friends with benefits. No that's just a way of getting their cake and eating it too. You never want to be led on. I don't care how much you like that person or see that person to be more than just a friend. If all the signs are friend signs, then trust me, that's all you are. Never let a man or woman use you to their advantage. They may have you playing the role of a girlfriend and actually just be their friend. You see, you have to be careful and be straight forward with what you want because you can just be playing a position which means they can easily change, and also, position is temporary. It has no future for you two, but when you have a purpose in someone's life, they value you, which means they plan on connecting with your spirit and not your flesh. You're in for the long run. It's not about what you can do for them. They actually want to know what they can do for you. Don't be a fool. You'll be living in a circle for years and still not have a purpose in that person's life.

That's why we don't do circles; we do triangles. Let's keep it real. We as singles play position more than enough so that we won't be alone, but if you really look at it, we are still alone. What's the purpose in having a man or woman when their heart isn't with you? Don't be anyone's dog on a leash, tailing you along for their own selfish reasons. You are worth more than what their eyes can see. A position gets you to the bedroom, but a purpose gets you to the altar. Don't settle, ladies and gentlemen. Don't confuse your position for your purpose because it's far different. Sometimes we start as a purpose because God is using us in that person's life. We stay longer than expected and become a position because what God wanted to use us for, he did, but we decided to stay longer. The other thing is when things don't work out, the heartache and pain make you see that we were in that person's life only for a season! Position versus purpose: know your role. Let God direct you in a person's life! Don't get caught up, Kingdom!

MESSAGE 17

Who You Mad At, Know Your Worth!

It's funny when we as people get out of a relationship, we tend to get bitter toward the person that hurt us. We go around telling all our friends and family how that person has hurt us, feeling sorry for ourselves, looking for others to agree with us, knowing that we played our part too, and blaming that person for wasting ten years of our lives. Can I just ask you something? Didn't God give you signs that he or she wasn't right for you? You know when he or she didn't come home at night and they lied they were to a friend's house or their mother's, well, that was your clue! When are you going to stop blaming and start praying? I'm not saying that person isn't wrong for hurting you in any kind of way? I'm simply saying how could that person know your worth if you yourself didn't because if you knew, you wouldn't have stayed for ten long years? Think! If you knew how valuable you were, you wouldn't have stayed with him the minute he stepped foot in your house saying he was coming from his momma or friend. No man or woman is worth your respect! If they had any for you, they wouldn't have cheated. So to get back to the message, *Who you are mad at!* Instead of telling to others and blaming him, go tell God how you feel and then start praying for yourself and pray for the person who had hurt you. Stop trying to prove yourself to a man, and stop trying to get them to validate you. How are they going to validate you? You're so busy validating them when they don't even know who they are. How does it look when a man with no purpose tells a woman with purpose that she's nothing? Be careful of people who judge you. They're not supposed to judge you anyway? Who are them to tell you right from wrong! Ladies, you are wasting your time giving the wrong man all of you and trying to make them see that you're the one when it might just be that you're not the one for them. You're fighting a never-ending battle, and it's not even yours; as a matter of fact, you're fighting the wrong battle! Your purpose is not in man. It's in God, so stop trying to fit in where you don't belong. You're forcing yourself in someone's life and they don't even want you there. (Get it together.) Only God knows your purpose. He had designed it, and the purpose God has for you is far greater than being a housewife to a man who knows nothing of your value! You're more than just pots, pans, clothes, cleaning, and cooking! You're trying to figure out where do you fit in his life, and guess what? He's trying to figure out how he can get you out of his life. I'm not trying to sound so mean because I've been here before. That's why I'm telling you what I know. Stop wasting your energy into an empty man. That's almost like pouring your energy in a small jar with a sealed top. Once you're in there and sealed, the only way you can get out is if he opens it. Ladies, he's not so. Keep yourself from pointless relationships. Seek to find purpose with God. He has a plan for your life. The Bible clearly states that a double-minded man is an unstable man in all his ways. This man can't get you anywhere but in trouble. I can promise you your purpose doesn't lie in man: it lies in Christ!

Poem 3

Love and Hip Hop

The feeling of butterflies the moment I heard your voice.

Love and Hip Hop I loved you the first time you asked me to give love another chance.

Writing poetry to each other relating to the fire we burned inside, words couldn't explain the feeling of belonging we both completed that in each other's life.

The smiles we brought to each other lives, I brought light to your path that seem so dim. The intimacy we shared it was one of a kind. I couldn't explain it because it was more than physical. It was mentally arousing. I couldn't think of any other person to be with than the man who stood before me.

Love and Hip Hop love couldn't define the reality of Hip Hop, because Hip Hop was accustomed to this harsh World. So instead of the two finding a solution, Love couldn't take a chance and lose her identity. Her walk meant the world to her, and Hip Hop couldn't find his way through the scene of life. But even though Hip Hop and Love decided to let the fire out, the reality still stands Love and Hip Hop has a rhythm that no other can maintain.

And deep down inside that fire still remains, it's just Love and Hip Hop are living some what seems to be the reason they're not as one. Identity and Image! Love and Hip Hop are living two different lives so the question still arises.

What could have been? What should have been? Is yet to be answered.

Love and Hip Hop!

MESSAGE 18

To the Left!

I named this Message "To the Left" because we as women give men too much authority over our lives, instead of God. Instead of us telling them to get going, we're holding on, and too what he has nothing in common with you. As a matter of fact, the minute you open up, Prince Charming will walk out the door, pass you by, and never turn back. So why are you waiting for him to change? Oh maybe if I let him see that I'm a good woman, he'll change! No! If he can't see it on his own, then, baby, why force him to see you? Ever heard the saying "Don't force it if it don't fit well". . . Ladies stop going in circles and for goodness stop listening to all that love music that has you all in emotions. Beyonce can sing crazy in love and all those other songs. She has her husband, and for what we can see, they are happy with each other! Our young women take those love songs to the heart and it keeps them in bondage because they think since the song has happy ending, their relationship will. Ladies, you have to seek God. Let God restore something's inside of you like that heart that has been broken, dreams that have been scattered, hopes that were crushed, and lies that were told. Women, if you're broken, stop looking and start seeking. There's no greater love like God's. Once you get a taste of his love, when a man comes your way with foolishness, you will recognize it. Ladies, we are fearfully and wonderfully made. Any man should feel honored to have us on their side. We shouldn't be dealing with any scrubs! It's time for women to know their worth and upgrade their status. We have been thought too much not to have the best. Our Father is the best. He told us we are to have nothing but the best! So, ladies, why are you settling for a Buick when you can have a Mercedes Benz? Come on, ladies, let's start telling these worldly men, "To the left!" Don't wait until he put you out on his birthday. Let him go! What God ordains God maintains, and if he hasn't maintained the relationship you're in, then it's not destined!

MESSAGE 19

A Breakup Is Like a Broken Mirror

Love can be dangerous if you're not careful of whom you're giving your heart too!

I title this chapter as "A breakup is like a broken mirror" simply because love can be dangerous. If you're not careful of whom you're giving your heart to, you can be setting yourself up for a heartache and pain. Sometimes people cling to you for their own selfish reasons. It might be because they can't find anyone else who is going to care for them like you do, or they might be holding on to you until they realize that you are the one. For whatever reasons they are holding on, if it's hurting you, don't wait for them to let go because they're not going to hold on as long as you do. Let's be real what man or woman wouldn't? No matter how long it takes for you to heal, don't settle for his or her games. When a mirror breaks into pieces, just think how hard it is to put it back together. Hard! It's almost impossible to fix it, and anyway, you don't want to fix a broken relationship because if it was meant, separation wouldn't exist. Yes, I know it's hard, and I have been through it. Believe me when I say it takes a lot of praying and devotion with God. You see, a lot of us today want what we want. Instead of spending time getting to know the Spiritual part of ourselves, we tend to put God to the side thinking we can fix what is broken. What happens then? You're left reminiscing about the good times, and then you catch yourself about to text his or her phone not realizing that there was a reason that those bad days outweigh those good. Don't get caught up in your emotions. Nothing hurts more than realizing that to the man who meant everything to you, you meant nothing to him. Well, one reason he couldn't appreciate you is because he was your everything and not God. We serve a jealous God. He wants us to put no man before him. It doesn't matter even if it's Obama! You're supposed to know that he is your only source. It's funny how it takes a couple of seconds to say, "Hello, I'm," but forever to say, "good-bye." You know the reason. Well, I'm glad you asked. I'm here to inform you the devil wants you to stay in a place where you can't produce and you can't elevate. He knows that if he can keep you where you're, then he can have you at a standstill where there's no moving in your life. Your identity is worth so much, and the enemy wants it. The devil wants us to think so low of ourselves because he stands for nothing! My pastor once preached a message and said, "The devil will try everything to stripe you from your identity, because he wants what you have." You see, he once had what you have, but he wanted to be more than the Creator! So he was casted down. Now you (Man) can get power and authority and not him because he has to ask God to do anything and everything, and when God says it's time to let go, he has to release you! Read about Job and see how the enemy tried everything to make Job curse God, but he didn't. Even his own wife told him to just curse God. That's why the devil likes to go to the woman first. That's what he did to Adam. He went to Eve instead of going straight to Adam because he's a coward. He goes through the backdoor instead of the front! Be careful not to pick up the pieces of your broken heart yourself because it's only going to cost you more pain and heartache. A relationship is like a glass; once it's broken, it's broken. There's no need to get your glue or tape. It's done! You never know why God delivered you from that person. One thing is for sure that person isn't destined to be in your future. Stop running behind him or her trying to make them see that you're the one. How do you know anyway that you are? If you have to go through all that, they really don't see your worth. You shouldn't have to force anyone to see you for who you are "What's understood should not be explained," so why are you hurting yourself? Take this time alone and minister to God. Let God restore the pieces back at least once. If God restores you, you will be made whole! Give your heart time to heal. Give your heart rest, please! There's nothing worse than a lifeless woman. Allow your Father to nurture your wound, and give it time to turn into a scar. No, you're not going to forget what he or she did, which is a good thing. That memory is going to keep you from making the same mistake. Don't get caught up with, "I miss him." What are you missing? The cheating, the cursing, and the belittling you. There's nothing to miss, ladies! I realize the worst way to love someone is to lay beside them every night knowing they don't love you, and you don't realize how much you care about someone until they show you they don't care about you. I'm going to end this message by saying something my pastor once told me, and it got stuck to me. "A man that loves you will pursue you. He will first love God and then you. He will also treat you like a queen. And most of all, he will not leave you during the storm."

MESSAGE 20

Admit It, Quit It, and Forget It!

So this message gets straight to the point. I read a book, and this was the title. I began to think how I could use this phrase to get through some of us. If you look spiritually, it's a powerful phrase. So I did some soul-searching, and this was what I came up with.

Admit it: Many of us never want to admit something that is painful or shameful. We want to keep it a secret and sweep it under the rug, but how many of you know that it's only for certain period that dirt is going to remain there and then it will be revealed? I want you to be naked and not to be ashamed. We don't want to deal with the pain that is keeping from where God is taking us. God dishonors a proud heart. He says, "Humble yourself and take up your cross." Let the real you show, so he can start stripping you from all the layers of rejection, hurt, pain, shame, and mistreatment, all which are hindering you from moving forward.

Quit it: You cannot continue to live in your past. It is dead. It's time to bury it, and when you go to the burial, don't grieve for too long because you're supposed to move on. Some breakups are never resolved. They are like walking dead. Inside of you, there's no life. Enough of all that. Everything that will not be healed must be forsaken, and to forsake, it is to forget it. God is telling you, you are to reckon as dead! Do not waste your time, body, or strength on that person. Romans Chapter 6:11–13 says, "Likewise reckon you also yourselves to be dead indeed unto sin, but alive unto God through Jesus Christ!" Just because you thought he was the one, it doesn't mean God doesn't know what he's doing. He's saving you actually from more disappointments, which is going to blind you from the man he wants in your life, so I say to you if it's easy for him to walk away from you, take it as he is doing you a big favor because a man that loves you won't walk away from you. Your destiny is to have some joy, and your joy is going to come from God, not man!

Forget it: Now forgetting what someone has done to you is not easy, but you don't have to live in the past hurt! When I say forget it, I don't mean be senile to what happened. I'm just saying don't dwell on it because you're blocking yourself. Release that pain from your memory. Let it go. Don't keep it because you might just miss your heaven! Allow God to heal you. Don't keep it inside and open another message before ending the first one. Follow these three steps: admit it, quit it, and forget it so that you can be the man or woman God has called you to be!

Poem 4
Stand

I stand for life.

I stand for joy.

I stand for respect.

If I stand for nothing, then I stand alone.

I stand for God.

I stand for trust.

I stand for honesty.

I stand for love 'cause if I stand for nothing, then I stand alone.

I stand for values.

I stand for dignity.

I stand for morals.

I stand for my rights.

If I stand for nothing, then I stand alone.

I stand to rejoice.

I stand for God's mercy.

I stand for God's grace, 'cause

If I stand for nothing, then I stand alone.

I stand to be loved.

I stand to be adored.

I stand to be married.

I stand to be the best in all areas of my life.

Once again, if I stand for nothing, I stand alone.

I stand for faith.

I stand for prosperity.

I stand for loyalty.

I stand for my Father in Heaven and for that I stand to survive!

MESSAGE 21

How Far Will You Go For the Man of God!

Those who are taught the word of God should
provide for their teachers sharing all good things
with them.(Gal. 6:6)

There're a lot of people out there in the world and also in the
church who think preachers are rich because of the church. Let
me just say the building is called the church, but the church is
us! A building cannot maintain itself without those who are
sitting in it. People mistakenly get it twisted thinking that "Oh,
I pay my tithes, so I am done with my job." Baby, let me tell you.
Your blessing is not tied up in your tithes; it is tied up in your
offerings. I was taught that your tithes are an obligation to Christ
because it states in the Bible to give your first fruits to god, so
after that it's offering. Your tithes are to pay the bills. Now what
about when there're plumbing problems, when a window breaks,
or when there're no cleaning supplies. That's where your offering
fits in. Know one thing, your pastor if he's Kevin Mitchell, I can't
speak for other pastors, is not using your money for his own
good. If anything, he's putting in for those who come up short
like me. I know sometimes all we have is our tithes. I'm saying if
you have extra, pour into the man of God. Help him to him us,

so his load won't be so heavy. We have to take of care the man of God like we take care of ourselves. That goes back to unity what he's always speaking on, so I just wanted to encourage you today and say how far will you go to take care of the man of God because he's not just any man. He's a man of the Most High, the Almighty, the alpha and Omega. He's the man of God! God bless you!!

MESSAGE 22

Will You Be There?

Galatians 6: 1–3 states, "Dear brothers and sister if another believer is overcome by some sin, you who are godly!" Not her or him, you who are godly should gently and humbly help that person back on to the right path. Now, it didn't say help that brother or sister get back onto the right path and then go gossip about what you had to do for that person to help them get back in the realm! It says gently and humbly, which means love and not judge because it could have been you! Okay, be careful not to fall into the same temptation yourself. Make sure you pray at all times because spirits do jump around. Be very cautious! Share each other's burdens, and in this way, obey the law of Christ. If you think you are too important to help someone, you are only fooling yourself because you are not that important! The body of Christ (the church) functions only when members work together for the common good. Now, that brings me to why our pastor says, "Unity is the key to keeping the kingdom together." His words are, "United we stand, united we fall!" Unity, it's not "u" and "t." It's wholeness "un" "Ity," which means, you have the "Ity" to make the word whole! Suppose you know someone who needs help, correction, and encouragement. If you gossip about that person and talk how awful he or she is for their sin to the next sister or brother who might just be going through the same thing, the person you are talking to would start thinking about giving up. Thus, you have done enough to spread that virus, and now, the person to whom you talked to is scared to come out of that bondage because of how you reacted to the other brother or sister. When you gossip about someone, you are spreading virus and causing people who are lost in their sin to stay closed! The Bible says gently and humbly reach out to that person offering to lift his or her load! So to end this message, remember, don't get caught up in yourself to where you think you can't backslide because the enemy is always on the move. If you're not in the will of God, he might just catch you sleeping! Help one another. We are here to uplift, encourage, and bring others close or closer to Christ! So my question to you is "Will you be there?"

MESSAGE 23

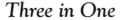

Three in One

I wrote this chapter because I wanted to reflect on how God can deliver you from things that will hinder your walk if you're serious about it and in the terms of Bishop Lloyd, "You want to get the hell out of it." Well, I once prayed to God and asked him to deliver me from my lustful ways. All it was doing was getting me into trouble, and I didn't find the love I was seeking. So as time went on, I continued praying for that deliverance because I knew God has a purpose for my life and he couldn't use me until I get it right. You know, how could I preach to someone about not having sex and having it myself? I would be fake! So I had to get this Spirit remove from me because God couldn't effectively use me as that's a bad spirit to have especially when you're single! To get back to the message, I had asked God to deliver me from a relationship that I was in then. I began to add to my prayer, "Lord, give me the strength to let go." You see, you can let go of something physically and still be holding on to it in your mind. "How's that?" you ask. Well, I'm glad you asked. You're still holding on to the memories, and you're still constantly worrying about what he's doing or where he is. The relationship I was asking for deliverance from was distracting my walk. Ladies, I'm here today to say, "God deliver 3 in 1." He delivered me from three negative things that was ruining my walk all at once! I was telling this story to my bestie (best friend), and at first, she couldn't understand me, but then when I read my prayer to her, she began to tell me about her three in one, which was her ungodly relationship she stayed in for tens, smoking weed, and drinking. The Lord took all three from her all at the same time, and she never looked back to say, "Well, how did I get out of this?" She knew that it was only her Father that could do that all at once. You know sometimes, it is a process for some of us and is kind of long, but nope, not for her. Don't get me wrong, delay is not a bad thing. Sometimes God wants us to stay a little longer just to make sure we don't go back, and then some of us are weaker than others, so he gets us out of that situation as quickly as possible. Then my bestie went on to say, "Sis, the Father, the Son, and the Holy Spirit, the Trinity! They all are Three In One." Then, she stated, "God delivered us from it all three. He made us brand-new. We divorced ourselves and married our Spirits!" Praise him, nobody but the Almighty who can do that! Praise him! So ladies and gentlemen, I end this message by saying if you want to get the hell out of something, you have to be willing to ask and move on it! Standing in the same position won't change anything!

MESSAGE 24

Don't Allow Fear to Rob You!

We as Christians are protected from demonic power (1 Pet. 5:8), particularly the spirit of fear. That is why we use the word of God to maintain our life. That's where the fighting of faith steps in. 1 Timothy 6:12 states, "Fight the good fight of faith, lay hold on eternal life, where unto thou art also called, and hast professed a good profession before many witnesses."

The enemy is always trying to steal our faith or at least render it ineffective. We have a choice to accept or resist his presence in our lives. As Christians, we don't have to deal with the enemy's tricks alone. We have the most powerful weapon in the world, and that's the word! In Matthew 14: 22–31, we read how peter's faith was tested. The minute he allowed the winds to distract him, he started sinking. That's how some of us are today. We see God. We know it's him. When we test him and ask him to prove himself to us, he does and still, we allow things to distract us from the assignment God has brought our way. One thing that I have learned about faith is that it's an action you have it in order for God to move. Our Father said, he would never leave us nor forsake us, so why are we constantly questioning his motives? Don't allow your mind to take you where your spirit isn't willing to dwell, for we know God has not given us a spirit of fear but a spirit of a sound mind. So, I encourage you, kingdom, don't allow fear to rob you from where God is trying to take you.!

Poem 5
This Can't Be Real!

Over and Over again I tell myself, "This can't be real!"

This feeling I can't resist, makes me want to scream!

Over and over again I tell myself, "This can't be real!"

This joy and peace I have; I have never had it before.

This smile that I have, I can't stop it! Over and over again, I tell myself "This can't be real!" This feeling of true love and this feeling of being worthy. Never in a million, I didn't think joy exists. I was just about to give up; I was just about to give in! "But God" is what I like to say, "But God!" He came to my rescue. He saw my SOSM (Someone Save Me)! And my life hasn't been the same. Never thought my life would be filled with so much joy, peace, and God! Over and over again, I tell myself, "This can't be real!"